A Small-Group Bible Study Series

Great Women of the Bible

Eve, Sarah, Rebekah, Leah, and Rachel

CONCORDIA PUBLISHING HOUSE • SAINT LOUIS

1 2 3 4 5 6 7 8 9 10   17 16 15 14 13 12 11 10 09 08

Contents

Hymnal Key

LSB = Lutheran Service Book
ELH = Evangelical Lutheran Hymnary
CW = Christian Worship
LW = Lutheran Worship
LBW = Lutheran Book of Worship
TLH = The Lutheran Hymnal

About This Series

Do you realize how often women are mentioned in the Bible? Do names like Eve, Sarah, Deborah, Ruth, Esther, Mary the mother of Jesus, Anna, Mary and Martha, Lydia, and Eunice and Lois sound familiar? They should. These are only a few of the great women mentioned in Holy Scripture.

The Bible not only gives us the names of these great women, but also describes their sorrows and joys, their defeats and victories, their intense private moments and important public duties. In contrast to the inaccurate myth that the Bible is an antiquated piece of antiwoman (misogynistic) literature, the Bible portrays women as God's creatures, different yet fully equal with men, fallen in sin yet redeemed by the precious blood of the Lamb.

In addition to sharing the thoughts, dreams, words, and deeds of women in the past, the Bible also provides helpful instruction for women of today. It encourages thrift and industry (Proverbs 31:10–31), teaches about healthy relationships between husbands and wives (Ephesians 5:22–33; Colossians 3:18–19), provides instruction in the relationship between older and younger women (Titus 2:3–5), celebrates the equality in diversity among believers (Galatians 3:28–29), and extols the important and varied roles women play in the partnership of the Gospel (Philippians 4:3).

Women can learn much about themselves in the Bible. But it would be a mistake to assume that what the Bible teaches about women is of no importance to men. In His Word, God unfolds for the believer both true womanhood and true manhood as He designed them, so that both sexes are affirmed in their equality and in their differences as God created them.

In this series, we cannot learn all there is to know about every great woman of the Bible. However, as we study God's Word, we can learn much about ourselves and our gracious Lord and how He worked in the lives of the great women of the Bible.

Suggestions for Small-Group Participants

1. Before you begin, spend some time in prayer asking God to strengthen your faith through a study of His Word. The Scriptures were written so that we might believe in Jesus Christ and have life in His name (John 20:31).

2. Even if you are not the small-group leader, prior to the meeting, take some time to look over the session, read the Bible verses, and answer the questions.

3. As a courtesy to others, be sure to arrive at each session on time.

4. Be an active participant. (The leader is there to facilitate group discussion, not give a lecture.)

5. Avoid dominating the conversation by answering each question or by giving unnecessarily long answers. Avoid the temptation to not share at all.

6. Treat anything shared in your group as confidential until you have asked and received permission to share it outside of the group. Treat information about others outside of your group as confidential until you have asked and received permission to share it inside of your group.

7. Realize that some participants may be new to the group or new to the Christian faith. Help them to feel welcomed and comfortable.

8. Affirm other participants when you can. If another participant offers what you perceive to be a "wrong" answer, ask the Holy Spirit to guide that person to seek the correct answer from God's Word.

9. Keep in mind that the questions are discussion starters. Don't be afraid to ask additional questions that relate to the session. Avoid getting the group off track.

10. If you feel comfortable doing so, now and then volunteer to pray either at the beginning or at the conclusion of the session.

Suggestions for Small-Group Leaders

1. Before you begin, spend some time in prayer asking God to strengthen your faith through a study of His Word. The Scriptures were written so that we might believe in Jesus Christ and have life in His name (John 20:31). Also, pray for participants by name.

2. See the Leader Guide at the back of this study. It will help guide you in discovering the truths of God's Word. It is not, however, exhaustive nor is it designed to be read aloud during your session.

3. Prior to your meeting, familiarize yourself with each session by reviewing the session material, reading the Bible passages, and answering the questions in the spaces provided. Your familiarity with the session will give you confidence as you lead the group.

4. As a courtesy to participants, begin and end each session on time.

5. Have a Bible dictionary or similar resource handy in order to look up difficult or unfamiliar names, words, and places. Ask participants to help you in this task. Be sure that each participant has a Bible and a study guide.

6. Ask for volunteers to read introductory paragraphs and Bible passages. A simple "thank you" will encourage them to volunteer again.

7. See your role as a conversation facilitator rather than as a lecturer. Don't be afraid to give participants time to answer questions. By name, thank each participant who answers, then ask for other participants. For example, you may say, "Thank you, Maggie. Would anyone else like to share?"

8. Now and then, summarize aloud what the group has learned by studying God's Word.

9. Keep in mind that the questions provided are discussion starters. Allow participants to ask questions that relate to the session. However, keep discussions on track with the session.

10. Everyone is a learner! If you don't know the answer to a question, simply tell participants that you need time to look at more

Scripture passages, or to ask your pastor, director of Christian education, or other lay leader. You can provide an answer at the next session.

11. Begin each session with prayer. Conclude each session with prayer. Ask for volunteers for these duties, and thank them for their participation. A suggested hymn is included at the end of each session. You may choose another hymn or song if you wish.

12. Encourage participants to read or reread the Scripture passages provided at the end of the session and, as they have time, to commit passages to memory.

❧
Eve

Any study of the great women of the Bible must begin with Eve. While many of Eve's experiences were similar to what today's women experience (relationships, work, home life), Eve's life was different from that of any other woman.

All we know about Eve is recorded in the Bible (see Genesis 2:18–4:25; 2 Corinthians 11:3; 1 Timothy 2:13). The Bible tells us how Eve came into this world, how she became the first human being to fall into sin, and how faith in the promised Savior gave her comfort and hope in her life. Let's look at what the Bible has to say about Eve and how God showed her His love and grace.

Eve before the Fall

When God created Adam, the first man, He used dust from the ground, breathing into him the breath of life (see Genesis 2). When God created Eve, the first woman, He took one of Adam's ribs (in Hebrew, part of his side) and fashioned her from it.

1. Read Genesis 1:27; Psalm 17:15; Ephesians 4:24; and Colossians 3:10. Like Adam, Eve was created in God's image. In what does this image consist?

2. Eve had no mother, older sister, or other female role model in her life. Do you think that she was disadvantaged by this? What common experiences do we have today that Eve never enjoyed?

3. Why was Eve created (Genesis 2:18; see also 1 Corinthians 11:3–9)? What do we learn about marriage in Genesis 2:24 and Matthew 19:3–9?

4. How did Adam and Eve spend their time in Eden (Genesis 2:8–17)? Why did God forbid them to eat the fruit of one certain tree?

Eve as a Sinner

Genesis 3 records the saddest event that ever happened on earth: humanity's fall from original righteousness (a right standing with God and with each other) into sin.

5. How was Eve involved in this great tragedy (Genesis 3:1–6; see also Romans 5:12)? Why did Satan succeed in bringing about humankind's fall?

6. How are Eve and Adam responsible for the entry of sin into the world (1 Timothy 2:14; see also Hosea 6:7)?

7. Eve and Adam showed that their love for each other was no longer pure and holy (Genesis 3:7). What are other ways sin affects our relationships with others, particularly those we love?

8. Sin changed Eve and Adam, which was evidenced by a change in their outward behavior (Genesis 3:7–10). What did they do instead of confessing their sins and seeking God's forgiveness (vv. 10–13)? How is this true of people even today?

9. How did the fall of Eve and Adam affect their future life (vv. 16–19)? the whole human race (Romans 5:12)? all living creatures (Romans 8:20–22)?

10. How were women, in particular, affected by sin (Genesis 3:16)? How does the Gospel of Jesus Christ encourage women in spite of the difficulties in this life (Galatians 3:26–29; Romans 8:18)? What special challenges and blessings do contemporary Christian women face today?

Eve as a Believer

Because of their rebellion against God, their Creator, Eve and Adam were expelled from the Garden of Eden (Genesis 3:22–24). Nevertheless, God offered them comfort and hope in the form of a promise.

11. Even as He cursed the serpent, God promised to Eve and Adam a coming Savior from sin (Genesis 3:15). To what other great woman of the Bible does this text point (see Matthew 1:18–25)?

12. How did Adam express his faith in this Gospel promise (Genesis 5:20)? What does the name *Eve* mean?

13. How did Eve show that she believed God's promise (Genesis 4:1)? How was God's image restored in Eve and Adam and, ultimately, all believers (Romans 8:29; 1 Corinthians 15:49; 2 Corinthians 3:18; Colossians 3:9–11)?

14. Is it fair to assume that Eve was the mother of many children (Genesis 5:4)? Why did she get to see many generations of descendants (Genesis 5:5)?

15. As Christians, what lessons can we learn from Eve's life?

Other Women of the Ancient World

16. Read Genesis 4:17 and Acts 17:26. The Bible records that Eve's sons married their sisters. Why were such marriages permissible at that time? Why were they forbidden later (Leviticus 18:6–18)?

17. A man named Lamech (LAH-mek) introduced the practice of marrying two wives (bigamy; Genesis 4:19–24). What is marriage according to God's design (Matthew 19:4–5)?

18. Because of humanity's sin, God used a great flood to destroy all human life except for eight people: Noah, his wife, and his sons and their wives (Genesis 6:1–7:13). How does this sad story nevertheless end on a note of promise (Genesis 8:15–22; see also 1 Peter 3:18–25)?

Closing Worship

Close by reading/singing together the words of *In Adam We Have All Been One* (*LSB* 569; *LW* 292; *LBW* 372; *CW* 396; *ELH* 431).

In Adam we have all been one,
One huge rebellious man;
We all have fled that evening voice
That sought us as we ran.

We fled Thee, and in losing Thee
We lost our brother too;
Each singly sought and claimed his own;
Each man his brother slew.

But Thy strong love, it sought us still
And sent Thine only Son
That we might hear His Shepherd's voice
And, hearing Him, be one.

O Thou who, when we loved Thee not,
Didst love and save us all,
Thou great Good Shepherd of mankind,
O hear us when we call.

Send us Thy Spirit, teach us truth;
Thou Son, O set us free
From fancied wisdom, self-sought ways,
To make us one in Thee.

Then shall our song united rise
To Thine eternal throne,
Where with the Father evermore
And Spirit Thou art one.

Martin H. Franzmann (1907–76)
© 1969 Concordia Publishing House

For Daily Bible Reading

Monday: Genesis 1 and 2
Tuesday: Genesis 3 and 4
Wednesday: Genesis 5 and 6
Thursday: Genesis 7 and 8
Friday: Genesis 9 and 10
Saturday: Proverbs 31:10–31
Sunday: Psalm 128
For memorization: Genesis 1:27; 2:18, 24; 3:15;
Proverbs 18:22

Sarah

While Eve was the first woman and is called the "Mother of All Living," Sarah is the most prominent woman in the Old Testament. She is called "Mother of God's Chosen People," "Mother of the Faithful," and "Mother of All Believers." The New Testament points to Sarah as a shining example of faith and as a role model for Christian women. Between Eve and the Virgin Mary, Sarah is the only woman God promises to become a foremother of Christ.

We should get to know Sarah, or Sarai (SAY-rye) as she was known in early life. Genesis 11:29–23:20 presents a fairly detailed biography of her. Additionally, let's look at some of the many references to Sarah in other passages of the Old and New Testaments.

Sarai and the Move to Canaan

Read Genesis 11:29–13:18. Abram (AY-bram) took Sarai to be his wife. Terah (TEAR-uh), Abram's father, led Abram, Sarai, and Lot (Terah's grandson) from Ur of the Chaldees (KAL-dees) as far as Haran. (If possible, consult a map of ancient Bible lands for these locations.)

19. Read Genesis 20:12. How was Sarai related to Abram before her marriage to him? Why did they live for a while at Haran?

20. God made a wonderful promise to Abraham regarding the promised Messiah (Genesis 12:3; see also 18:18; 22:18). Abram demonstrated his faith in this promise (Genesis 12:4–5). How did Sarai likewise demonstrate her faith in her coming Savior (1 Peter 3:1–6; see also Hebrews 11:1–2)?

21. Because of a severe famine, Sarai and Abram left Canaan for Egypt (Genesis 12:10–20). How did Abram put Sarai's love to a severe test? What did God do to prevent Abram's scheme from becoming a tragedy (vv. 17–20)? What can we learn from this?

22. After they returned from Egypt, God made Sarai and Abram very wealthy (Genesis 13:1–2). Why does the promise that God gave to Abram also apply to Sarai (v. 16)?

Sarai's Desire for a Child

Read Genesis 15:1–17. God repeated His promise to Abram and his family to give him a son and many offspring, sealing His promise with a covenant of blood.

23. Sarai concluded that God had made her unable to conceive and give birth (Genesis 16:1–5). Was it faith or doubt that caused Sarai and Abram to use Hagar (HAY-gar), Sarai's maidservant, to provide an offspring? What was the result?

24. Why did God change Abram and Sarai's names to Abraham and Sarah (Genesis 17:1–8, 15–21)? What caused Abraham to laugh when God promised him and Sarah a son (v. 17)? What would be their son's name (v. 19)?

25. Sarah and Abraham entertained three heavenly visitors (Genesis 18:1–15). When the Lord promised that Sarah would give

birth to a son, she laughed (Genesis 18:12). When are we most likely to doubt God's Word?

Sarah as a Happy Mother

Read Genesis 21:1–7. God was faithful to His promise: Sarah gave birth to a son, Isaac. Isaac's name means "he laughs."

26. Sarah's laughter now (vv. 6–7) was different from her laughter earlier (Genesis 18:12). Describe those times when have you been overjoyed with God's amazing work in your life.

27. Read Genesis 21:8–21. Why was Sarah justified in having Hagar and Ishmael sent away (vv. 12–13; see also Galatians 4:29–30)? What difficult decisions must Christian parents today make on behalf of their children?

28. Read Genesis 22:1–19. How do you think Sarah responded when Abraham took Isaac to be sacrificed? when they returned safe and sound? To what article of faith did Sarah and Abraham cling (v. 5)?

Sarah's Death and Burial

Read Genesis 23:1–20. Out of all the women in the Bible, Sarah is the only one whose age at her death is given: 127 years.

29. How was Abraham affected by Sarah's death (v. 2)? Describe her burial place (vv. 17, 19). What does Abraham's purchase of this property in Canaan indicate? What does your congregation do, or what can it do, to help those who are grieving over a loss?

30. Who besides Sarah would be buried there (see Genesis 25:9–10; 35:28–29; 49:29–32; 50:12–14)? How was Isaac affected by his mother's death (see Genesis 24:67)? To what hope do we cling when death takes away from us a believing loved one (see Job 19:25–27; Romans 6:3–5)?

Other Biblical References to Sarah

31. The prophet Isaiah calls Sarah our spiritual mother (Isaiah 51:1–2). Who are the women in your life who have either brought you faith or have strengthened your faith?

32. Sarah and Abraham's true children are those who believe in Jesus Christ, the promised Seed and Messiah (Romans 9:6–9). How does your spiritual connection to these ancient people of faith impact your Christian life today?

33. Paul refers to Sarah as a "free woman" (Galatians 4:22–31). Why is it important to remember that, like our spiritual mother, we are saved by God's grace through faith in God's promises and not by our good works?

34. Both Sarah and Abraham believed that God would be faithful to His promise (Hebrews 11:11). What promises in God's Word do you find particularly comforting and why?

35. Sarah was a model wife (1 Peter 3:1–6). What are other attributes of great women of faith (see Galatians 5:22–23)?

Other Women of That Period

Hagar was Sarah's servant who bore Abraham a son, Ishmael.

36. God promised Hagar that she would have a son (Genesis 16:11–12. In spite of her disagreements with Sarah, was Hagar a believer (v. 13)?

37. Discuss the tragic story of Lot's wife (Genesis 19:12–26; see also Luke 17:32). Why must we always be on guard against temptation?

38. Lot's daughters committed incest with their father (Genesis 19:30–38). His eldest daughter's son, Moab, would become an ancestor of Ruth (Ruth 1:1–4). Who is Ruth's most famous descendant (see Ruth 4:21–22; Matthew 1:1, 5–6, 16)?

39. Following Sarah's death, Abraham married Keturah (Genesis 25:1–4). What does Paul suggest for Christian widows or widowers (1 Corinthians 7:8–9, 39)?

Closing Worship

Close by reading/singing together the words of *The God of Abr'ham Praise* (*LSB* 798:1–4, 8–9; *LW* 450; *TLH* 40; *LBW* 544; *ELH* 69).

The God of Abr'ham praise, Who reigns enthroned above;
Ancient of everlasting days And God of love.
Jehovah, great I AM! By earth and heav'n confessed;
I bow and bless the sacred name Forever blest.

The God of Abr'ham praise, At whose supreme command
From earth I rise and seek the joys At His right hand.
I all on earth forsake, Its wisdom, fame, and pow'r,
And Him my only portion make, My shield and tow'r.

The God of Abr'ham praise, Whose all-sufficient grace
Shall guide me all my pilgrim days In all my ways.
He deigns to call me friend; He calls Himself my God.
And He shall save me to the end Through Jesus' blood.

He by Himself has sworn; I on His oath depend.
I shall, on eagle wings upborne, To heav'n ascend.
I shall behold His face; I shall His pow'r adore
And sing the wonders of His grace Forevermore.

The God who reigns on high The great archangels sing,
And "Holy, holy, holy!" cry, "Almighty King!"
Who was and is the same And evermore shall be:
Jehovah, Father, Great I AM! We worship Thee!"

The whole triumphant host Give thanks to God on high.
"Hail, Father, Son, and Holy Ghost!" They ever cry.
Hail, Abr'ham's God and mine! I join the heav'nly lays:
All might and majesty are Thine And endless praise!

Thomas Olivers (1725–99), alt.
Public domain

For Daily Bible Reading

Monday: Genesis 11:27–13:18
Tuesday: Genesis 14–16
Wednesday: Genesis 17–18
Thursday: Genesis 19–20; 1 Peter 3:1–7
Friday: Genesis 21–22
Saturday: Genesis 23 and 25
Sunday: Ephesians 5:17–33
For memorization: Genesis 16:13; 18:19; 22:18;
Hebrews 11:13, 16; 1 Peter 3:4–6

Rebekah

Rebekah, the daughter-in-law of Sarah, is another great woman whose story we should know. The most interesting part of Rebekah's life is told in Genesis 24. Truly, she was an "answer to prayer," indeed many prayers; she played a vital role in God's history of salvation. Rebekah's life highlights God's grace and His commitment to His promise of our salvation working in our lives, even when we do not live fully according to His will. By God's grace and choosing, Rebekah was also a foremother of Christ (Matthew 1:2; see also Romans 9:10–11). Let's look at the life and times of Rebekah.

Rebekah's Courtship and Marriage

Read Genesis 24:1–27. Following Sarah's death, Abraham was advanced in years and concerned about Isaac's future. Isaac was forty years old (Genesis 25:20) and had not yet found a suitable bride.

40. Why was Abraham concerned about the religion of his future daughter-in-law? What benefits does a shared faith bring to a marriage?

41. Abraham believed that a suitable spouse for Isaac could be found only in Haran (see Genesis 22:20–24). Ultimately, why was Eliezer (el-ee-AY-zer), Abraham's chief servant, successful in encountering Rebekah there (Genesis 24:7, 12–14, 24–27)?

42. What is surprising about the way in which Eliezer met Rebekah at the well (24:15)? Why did Eliezer believe that Rebekah was the right spouse for Isaac?

43. Eliezer was cordially received in Rebekah's home (Genesis 24:29–33, 50–51, 57–58). How did Rebekah's parents recognize that this union was under the Lord's direction? Ultimately, who made the final decision regarding the marriage proposal?

44. Where did Rebekah meet Isaac for the first time, and what was her reaction (Genesis 24:61–67)? How is their marriage described (v. 67)?

Rebekah as a Wife and Mother

Read Genesis 25:19–34. Sadly, for twenty years, Rebekah and Isaac were childless. God's heart was doubly moved, however, by prayers for a son (v. 21). God gave Isaac and Rebekah twins: Esau (who was born first, and thus was the eldest) and Jacob.

45. Which of Rebekah's sons did the Lord designate to bear the messianic promise (v. 23)?

46. As Esau and Jacob grew older, they displayed different personality characteristics (v. 27). Did Isaac and Rebekah tend to play favorites (v. 28)? What can Christian parents do to ensure that their time and devotion are shared fairly among their children?

47. Read Genesis 26:1–11. How did Rebekah and Isaac's deception mirror that of Sarah and Abraham (see Genesis 20)? How can we learn both from our parents' good example as well as their mistakes?

48. Much to the dismay of his mother and father, Esau married unbelieving Hittite women (Genesis 26:34–35). Why should we consider our faith when making important decisions?

49. Sadly, Rebekah resorted to trickery in order to obtain the blessing for her son (Genesis 27:1–41). How could Rebekah have helped Jacob obtain his father's blessing without using such means?

50. In this instance, Jacob would not have sinned had he disobeyed his mother (see Acts 5:29). List other examples where we must obey God rather than even legitimate authority figures.

51. Both Rebekah and Jacob suffered consequences because of their deception (Genesis 27:42–28:5). How can we be assured of God's forgiveness in Christ, even when we don't feel forgiven (see Psalm 103:10–12; Ephesians 1:7; 1 John 4:9–10)?

52. What lessons may Christian women learn from Rebekah's life?

Other Women of That Period

53. Read Genesis 35:8. What do we learn about Rebekah's nurse?

54. Who were Esau's wives (Genesis 26:34; 28:8–9; 36:1–8)? How does the Bible describe them?

Closing Worship

Close by reading/singing together the words of *Go, My Children, with My Blessing* (*LSB* 922; *CW* 332).

Go, My children, with My blessing, Never alone.
Waking, sleeping, I am with you; You are My own.
  In My love's baptismal river
    I have made you Mine forever.
Go, My children, with My blessing—You are My own.

Go, My children, sins forgiven, At peace and pure.
Here you learned how much I love you, What I can cure.
  Here you heard My dear Son's story;
    Here you touched Him, saw His glory.
Go, My children, sins forgiven, At peace and pure.

Go, My children, fed and nourished, Closer to Me;
Grow in love and love by serving, Joyful and free.
  Here My Spirit's power filled you;
    Here His tender comfort stilled you.
Go, My children, fed and nourished, Joyful and free.

I the Lord will bless and keep you And give you peace;
I the Lord will smile upon you And give you peace:
    I the Lord will be your Father,
        Savior, Comforter, and Brother.
Go, My children; I will keep you And give you peace.

Jaroslav J. Vajda (b. 1919)
© 1983 Concordia Publishing House

∽

For Daily Bible Reading

Monday: Genesis 24
Tuesday: Genesis 25
Wednesday: Genesis 26
Thursday: Genesis 27:1–40
Friday: Genesis 27:41–28:22
Saturday: 1 Timothy 2
Sunday: Hebrews 11:1–20
For memorization: Proverbs 12:4; 29:15; 31:30;
Romans 15:4; Ephesians 4:25; 5:33

❧
Leah and Rachel

The names of Leah and Rachel, who not only were sisters but also Rebekah's daughters-in-law, may be familiar to participants. Leah and Rachel's story is a bittersweet one. Although married to the same man, which was the permitted custom at that time, one was not loved by him. However, we are primarily interested in learning what kind of women Leah and Rachel were. If you've studied their lives before, what do you remember about Leah and Rachel? Did your study leave you with any impressions about them? In this session, we will review the lives of Leah and Rachel and apply to our own lives what we learn through the study of God's Word.

Leah: Unloved but Full of Praise

Read Genesis 29:1–20. Having been sent by his father, Isaac, Jacob traveled to Paddan Aram, the ancestral land of his mother, Rebekah. Jacob met Rachel at the well; he was overcome with emotion as he learned that he had reached his destination.

55. Jacob had no intention of marrying Leah, but she nevertheless became his wife (Genesis 29:21–31). Did Jacob treat Leah as a husband should (vv. 30–31)? What are some of the causes of unhappiness in marriage?

56. God partially compensated Leah for her loveless husband by giving her children (vv. 31–35). In spite of her unhappy circumstances, how did Leah show that she trusted in our gracious God?

26

57. Following the custom of the time, Leah and Rachel urged Jacob to marry their servants in order to produce heirs (Genesis 30:1–16). What did Leah do to draw Jacob away from Rachel (vv. 14–16)? As Christians, why should we be on guard when we experience powerful emotions, especially love?

58. Leah gave birth to six sons and a daughter, Dinah (Genesis 29:31–35; 30:17–21). What special promise did her son Judah bear (Genesis 49:10; see also Matthew 1:1–3, 16)? When did Leah die, and where was she buried (Genesis 49:31)?

Rachel: Beloved but Unhappy

Review Genesis 29:1–30. It is quite possible that Jacob fell in love with Rachel at first sight.

59. Jacob's preference for Rachel was due to her outward appearance (v. 17); he even worked seven additional years to marry her (vv. 18–20; 26–27) Should we blame Jacob for loving Rachel more than Leah (v. 30)?

60. In spite of her husband's love, Rachel's childlessness made her unhappy (Genesis 29:31). How were Rachel's prayers finally answered (Genesis 30:22–24)? Why should Christians "pray without ceasing" (1 Thessalonians 5:17; see also John 14:13; 15:16)?

61. Rachel stole her father's idols (Genesis 31:19, 30–35). What finally became of them (Genesis 35:1–4)? How easy is it to

slip into sinful behavior when confronted with a familiar temptation?

62. Sadly, Rachel died giving birth to Benjamin (Genesis 35:16–20). How did Jacob show that his love for Rachel never waned (Genesis 37:3; 42:4)? How did Jesus show that He was and is fully devoted to His bride, the Church (Ephesians 5:24-26)?

Other Women of That Period

63. Bilhah (Genesis 30:3–8) and Zilpah (vv. 9–13) were Rachel and Leah's servants and mothers to Jacob's children. In Genesis 37:2, they are called Jacob's "wives." Why is respect and love especially called for in blended families?

64. Tragically, Shechem raped Leah's daughter, Dinah. In response, her brothers Simeon and Levi killed Shechem and his father (Genesis 34:1–4, 25-26). Of what should Christians beware when angry, even when that anger is justified (Ephesians 4:26)?

65. What are we told about Judah's wife (Genesis 38:1–5, 12)? Why might God want us to know that Tamar is a foremother of Christ (see Matthew 1:3)?

66. Potiphar's wife unsuccessfully tried to seduce Joseph (Genesis 39:1, 7–20). What does God promise us when we are faced with temptation (1 Corinthians 10:13)?

67. Joseph married Asenath, the daughter of a pagan Egyptian priest (Genesis 41:45, 50–52). What encouragement does God offer to Christian spouses if their wives or husbands are not believers (1 Corinthians 7:13–15)?

Closing Worship

Close by reading/singing together the words of *The King of Love My Shepherd Is* (*LSB* 709; *LW* 412; *TLH* 431; *LBW* 456; *CW* 375; *ELH* 370).

The King of love my shepherd is,
Whose goodness faileth never;
I nothing lack if I am His
And He is mine forever.

Where streams of living water flow,
My ransomed soul He leadeth
And, where the verdant pastures grow,
With food celestial feedeth.

Perverse and foolish oft I strayed,
But yet in love He sought me
And on His shoulder gently laid
And home rejoicing brought me.

In death's dark vale I fear no ill
With Thee, dear Lord, beside me,
Thy rod and staff my comfort still,

Thy cross before to guide me.
Thou spreadst a table in my sight;
Thine unction grace bestoweth;
And, oh, what transport of delight
From Thy pure chalice floweth!

And so through all the length of days
Thy goodness faileth never;
Good Shepherd, may I sing Thy praise
Within Thy house forever!

Henry W. Baker (1821–77)
Public domain

For Daily Bible Reading

Monday: Genesis 29–30
Tuesday: Genesis 31–33
Wednesday: Genesis 34–35
Thursday: Genesis 37–39
Friday: Genesis 40–42
Saturday: Genesis 43–45
Sunday: Genesis 46–50
For memorization: Genesis 32:10; 39:9; 43:9; 49:10;
Matthew 2:18

Leader Guide

Each one-hour session is divided into three to six subsections. Participants will first look at the life of the historical figure in the biblical text. Then they will be encouraged from what they read and discuss to make practical application to their own lives and situations.

Remember that this study is only a guide. Your role as group leader is to facilitate interaction between individual participants and the biblical text and between participants in your small group. By God's Spirit working through His Word, participants will learn and grow together.

Begin and end each session with prayer. Each session concludes with suggestions for weekly Bible readings, Bible memorization, and a hymn. You may choose a different hymn or song based on the needs of your group.

Eve

Our study of the great women of the Bible naturally begins with Eve. Since Eve was the first woman, the study of her life may prove more interesting than that of any other woman. The Bible presents the historical facts about Eve's life. If participants are unfamiliar with her story, the leader could suggest Bible readings in advance of the session so that class time is not spent so much in reading the texts as in exploring them, discussing them in a group, and making personal application of them to our daily lives. In this session, the leader may assign Genesis 2–4.

Eve's life story may briefly be outlined according to these three periods: (1) Eve before the fall; (2) Eve as a sinner; and (3) Eve as a believer.

Eve before the Fall

Everything the Bible says about Eve in her state of innocence applies only to her and to no other woman. No woman has ever been sinless like Eve. Hence, no one can adequately conceive of the glory and experiences that must have been only hers. Apart from what God says about her in His Word, we can only try to imagine what Eve must have been like. Only when we are in heaven will we be able to understand what blessings Eve enjoyed while on earth.

1. God constructed Eve's body around bone and flesh of Adam (Genesis 2:23). This is highly significant and points to their equality as created human beings. Whether God used Adam's actual rib or part of his side to create Eve we do not know. Eve's creation is, of course, a miracle that human reason cannot explain. Even though Eve was created later than Adam, she, too, was created in the image of God (Genesis 1:27). According to Ephesians 4:24 and Colossians 3:10, the divine image consists in perfect innocence, purity, and holiness; in a blissful knowledge of God; and in intimate communion with God. The image resulted in physical and mental perfection. Vestiges or remnants of the image of God, such as the ability to reason or to exercise dominion over other creatures, still reside in human beings. However, because of sin these vestiges

or remnants do not exist in human beings in a state of perfection. Thus, sinful humankind cannot now be said to possess the divine image. Adam and Eve lost God's image in the fall. However, through the Gospel of Jesus Christ, God is restoring this image in believers.

2. Created in perfection, Eve could exist very well without many things that are so essential to our lives. She had no need for physical and mental growth, or to learn essential facts by means of trial and error. As God's perfect creature, Eve could adjust herself immediately to the life situations into which she had been placed. Everything on earth was hers for her use and enjoyment. Physically, she needed no change or improvement. It is possible that by God's will Eve's mental and spiritual powers could have become expanded indefinitely and enriched through experience. Allow participants to discuss whether or not they believe the lack of female role models was to Eve's disadvantage. Discussing contemporary human experiences may also help to contrast our lives today with Eve's life on earth so long ago.

3. Eve was created to be Adam's "helper" (Genesis 2:18), his complementary partner. Marriage and the relationship between husband and wife are articles of creation; they have not been abrogated by our redemption in Christ (1 Corinthians 11:3–9). All human beings were to be of one flesh and blood, united by a common tie. Eve, in particular, was to be the helper and wife of Adam and the mother of all human beings. Immediately after God created Eve, He instituted holy matrimony (Genesis 2:24). While on earth, the first marriage was certainly made in heaven! Allow participants to discuss marriage as God intends it, the one-flesh union of one man and one woman for life, which Jesus affirmed (Matthew 19:3–9).

4. God provided His whole creation to serve the pleasure and happiness of His human creatures. Their enjoyment of Paradise was heightened by the fact that it became the sphere of their creative and purposeful activity (Genesis 2:15–16). The Bible does not describe specific duties, but it does indicate that God desired Eve and Adam to tend to His garden. We do not know how long Adam and Eve lived in the garden in the state of innocence and blessedness, but the text does seem to indicate that the time between the creation of our first human parents and their fall was brief. Why would God forbid them to eat of one certain tree? So that Adam

and Eve would freely and voluntarily choose to serve God and remain loyal to Him. Thus, He gave them a test (Genesis 2:17). It was not God's fault that they failed to pass the test; they had the power to pass it.

Eve as a Sinner

5. The history of humankind would have been entirely different had our first parents, Eve and Adam, not fallen into sin! Think of it: no death, no disease, no despair. Although Eve was the first to sin by doubting God's Word and giving in to the serpent's suggestions, Adam is equally to blame. Generally, the Bible makes Adam responsible for sin and corruption (Romans 5:12). We know, however, why Satan succeeded, that is, why both Eve and Adam fell. They permitted Satan to turn them away from God and His Word and to plant seeds of doubt, distrust, unbelief, and pride into their hearts. The devil first approached Eve rather than Adam, who was created first, to bring disorder into God's orderly creation (see 1 Corinthians 14:33; 2 Corinthians 12:20; James 3:15–17).

6. Eve was the one "who was deceived" (1 Timothy 2:14), but Adam was "faithless" (Hosea 6:7). Both Eve and Adam are equally to blame for the fall. The Scriptures pronounce all human beings to be lost and condemned sinners in God's sight (Psalm 14:3; Romans 3:23). Eve made the first misstep and is responsible not only for her fall, but also for the fall of Adam and all their descendants. Eve's fall serves as a warning to all believers, female and male (2 Corinthians 11:3; see also 1 Corinthians 1:11–13).

7. Eve and Adam's estrangement from God due to their sin led quickly to their estrangement from each other. We see evidence of this in their desire to cover their naked bodies (Genesis 3:7), an indication that impure thoughts had now filled their hearts. Fortunately, their consciences had become sensitized and they felt ashamed. A certain amount of clothing is needed for protection, health, and comfort. But there is also a moral reason for keeping some parts of the human body covered; the fact that most people sense this obligation shows that people, even after the fall, retained some knowledge of the moral law, which was written into our hearts at creation. Allow participants to discuss other ways sin affects not only our relationship with God, but also with others. Ex-

34

amples might include hurtful words that cause an estrangement, deception that erodes trust between individuals, and so on.

8. We shouldn't be surprised at the aftereffects of sin. Adam and Eve's relationships and behaviors changed due to their transgression. They had become separated from God, and now they feared and hated Him. They did not seek His forgiveness or a desire to be reinstated in His favor. What did they do? They attempted to hide themselves and their sin from their Creator. Even when God called them to account, they tried to shirk personal responsibility for their fall: Adam blamed Eve and Eve blamed the serpent. In reality, both blamed God for having created them. Here we have a picture of human nature as it has been ever since the fall. Allow participants to discuss how we see these same sin-infected attitudes and actions today.

9. Genesis 3:16–19 briefly summarizes the lot of humankind under sin. How different from the promise Satan had made (Genesis 3:5)! Far from being like God, humankind had now lost the image of God. Before, Adam and Eve had had only happy and pleasant experiences; now they would experience everything that was evil and unpleasant. Their lives would be filled with sorrow, suffering, bitter toil, and disappointments. They would have to struggle and labor to supply their needs and preserve their lives. Didn't God threaten sinners with immediate death (Genesis 2:17)? Spiritually, Adam and Eve had died the very moment they fell (Ephesians 2:1). The germ of death had also become implanted in their bodies. It was due solely to God's grace that they were granted a long span of physical life, so that they might be restored again to spiritual life. The doors of the earthly Paradise were now closed to them, and all that it stood for was to remain lost to them in this world. Adam and Eve's sin is passed down to all of their descendants (Romans 5:12), except for our Savior, Jesus Christ. All living creatures, indeed the whole created universe, are under the bondage of sin and death and yearn for the return of Christ and the full restoration of God's created order (Romans 8:20–22; see also 2 Peter 3:13; Revelation 21:1).

10. This passage should be discussed with tact and sensitivity. Even if Adam and Eve had not fallen into sin, God's ordered differences between and spheres of influence for men and women would have remained (1 Timothy 2:13; 1 Corinthians 11:3–12). However, after the fall this ordering has become particularly burdensome due

to the influence of sin on human nature. In the history of humankind, women have especially suffered the results of sin, not only physically, but in many other aspects of their lives as well. In the home and in the Church, wives are obliged to respect the headship and authority of their husbands (see 1 Corinthians 14:34; 1 Timothy 2:13). However, spiritually women and men are equals in Christ before God (Galatians 3:26–29). In spite of our hardships, even those due to the influence of sin in the world around us, God gives us the courage to endure (Romans 8:18). Allow participants to discuss both the challenges and blessings contemporary Christian women face today. Examples may include finding the balance between work and home life, teaching children to make wise choices in a culture with different moral values, and so on.

Eve as a Believer

11. Eve and Adam must have felt intense sorrow when they were forced to leave the garden, knowing they could never return to it. Had it not been for the first Gospel promise (Genesis 3:15), their lives would have been filled with gloom and despair. In cursing the serpent, God announced the serpent's (Satan's) defeat: "He shall bruise [or crush] your head, and you shall bruise His [Jesus'] heal." This denoted both the crucifixion of our Lord and Savior Jesus Christ and His resurrection victory over sin, death, and the devil. We can be sure that God did not proclaim this first Gospel message to Eve and Adam in vain (Isaiah 55:11). Ultimately, this promise is fulfilled in part by another great woman of the Bible, the Virgin Mary ("the woman") and in full by our Savior, Mary's Son, Jesus Christ ("Offspring"; see Matthew 1:18–25).

12. The name that Adam gave his wife testified to his faith in the divine promise (Genesis 5:20). *Eve* means "living" or "life," so Eve is the "Mother of All Living." How could Adam give his wife such a name after God gave them their death sentence (v. 19)? Adam believed that sin would not be able to extinguish life and that life would win out in the end. As the mother of humankind, Eve was to him the symbol of life and hope that would be realized in the woman's Seed, Christ. The clothing with which God covered them (v. 21) taught them that God would cover their sins and hide them from His sight with the righteousness Christ would procure for them.

13. Eve clearly revealed what thoughts she cherished when she gave birth to her first child. *Cain* means "gotten" or "acquired." Eve looked upon her firstborn as a gift of God. But she expressed more than that. Not only did she now feel sure of God's grace, but she believed that God's promise (Genesis 3:15) had now been fulfilled and that her son would be the Messiah. According to the original Hebrew text, Eve said: "I have gotten a man, the Lord," which is how Martin Luther correctly translated this passage. Eve was anxious to have the messianic promise fulfilled at once. She firmly believed it would come true. Unfortunately, she had fixed her hope on the wrong person, as she discovered when this son grew up. She soon noticed how sinful and wicked he was, even before the great tragedy of murder was enacted in her family. Disappointed in the fulfillment of her hopes, she called her second son *Abel*, a name that means "vanity." But her hopes were revived again when Seth was born; she regarded him as a "substitute" for godly Abel (Genesis 4:25). Abel and Seth both were godly, but only because in them the religious teaching of their parents had been effective. Seth introduced public worship and preaching among the descendants of Adam.

Through faith in the coming Messiah, promised by God in Genesis 3:15, God in His grace began restoring His image in Adam and Eve. The same is true for all believers today (see Romans 8:29; 1 Corinthians 15:49; 2 Corinthians 3:18; Colossians 3:9–11).

14. We are not told how many children Eve had, but she was undoubtedly the mother of a large family (Genesis 5:4). Eve probably did not live as long as Adam (930 years; Genesis 5:5), but she may have lived five, six, or more centuries. At that early period, people lived simple lives, climatic conditions were favorable, and sin had not as yet weakened humankind as much as it did later. God, moreover, wanted His Word to be handed down orally to many generations through Adam and Eve. We can imagine Eve telling the story of her life in Eden to her great-great-grandchildren.

15. Through Eve, believers are warned against doubting God's Word or adding to it and of the awful results of sin in our relationship with God and those whom we love, particularly our spouses and family members. Nevertheless, the story of Eve is also one of great comfort, for even though Eve and Adam hid themselves from God when they had sinned, God in His grace pursued them in love to offer them His rich forgiveness through His Son, Jesus Christ,

our Lord. This they received through faith in the first Gospel promise (Genesis 3:15).

Other Women of the Ancient World

This last section contains supplementary material, which may be omitted if the story of Eve takes up the entire session.

16. Adam's sons had to marry their sisters or nieces; at the beginning this was in accordance with God's will (Genesis 4:17; see Acts 17:26). Later it became necessary to forbid such marriages for biological and social reasons (see Leviticus 18:6–18).

17. Lamech, the fifth generation of Cain, became the first person to marry multiple spouses (a bigamist or polygamist; Genesis 4:19). This was not and is not God's design for marriage, which is the one-flesh union of one man and one woman for life (Matthew 19:4–5).

18. Due to humankind's sin, God destroyed the world by the great flood. The only godly persons living at that time were Noah, his wife, his three sons, and his three daughters-in-law (Genesis 6:18; 7:7). The flood was disastrous for the overwhelming majority of people alive at the time; the true story of the flood serves as God's "new creation" (many of the same themes are found in Genesis 8 as in Genesis 1 and 2). According to Peter, the flood points forward in time to Holy Baptism, which "now saves you" (1 Peter 3:21), just as the flood waters, while drowning unbelievers below, actually saved Noah and his family by separating them from the Lord's wrath on earth. Baptism is a powerful means of grace, and those who believe and have been baptized (Mark 16:16) can be certain that they have been saved.

Sarah

Sarah's (Sarai's) life runs parallel to that of her husband, Abraham (Abram). If participants are familiar with Sarah's story, it may be unnecessary to devote more than a single one-hour session to discussing the story of this famous woman. However, the leader may wish to extend the session by supplementing the questions and answers in this session with additional material concerning Sarah's life.

Some may prefer to study the events in the life of Sarah in chronological order. Others may prefer to study Sarah's life topically. In such a case, a suggested topical arrangement may look like this: (1) Sarah—A Woman of Faith and Courage (Genesis 11:27–12:9); (2) How God Tested and Strengthened Sarah's Faith (Genesis 12:10–18:15); (3) How Sarah Gave Proof of a Strong Faith (Genesis 21:1–12). Like any great woman of the Bible, Sarah had her weaknesses. However, throughout her whole life, Sarah also showed that she was a humble and consecrated child of God.

Sarai and the Move to Canaan

19. Sarai was Abram's half sister, sharing with him the same father, Terah (Genesis 20:12). At this time in history (circa 2000 BC and later), marriage between such close relatives was still tolerated. In Abram's case, this arrangement is unsurprising because the Chaldeans were steeped in idolatry. Hence, it would have been impossible for Abram to find a woman of the true faith outside his family circle. Ur was so infested with idol worship that Terah was compelled (perhaps because of disgust or persecution) to seek a new home for his family elsewhere. From Joshua 24:2, it appears that Terah and other members of his family had worshiped idols at least for a time. Whether Abram and Sarai always worshiped the one, true God, we do not know.

Terah's family traveled about six hundred miles up the Euphrates River and established a colony in Mesopotamia, which they named Haran in honor of Abram's brother and Lot's father, who had died in Ur (see Genesis 11:27–32). The Bible does not say how long Abram and Sarai lived there. When they left Haran for Canaan, Abram was seventy-five years old and Sarai was sixty-five (Genesis 12:4).

20. God made a remarkable promise to Abram (and by extension to Sarai and all their descendants; Genesis 12:3; 18:18; 22:18). The most important part of this promise is its specific reference to Christ as Abram's descendant and the Savior of all human beings.

Many Christians know that Abram was a great man of faith, which he demonstrated many times in his life, including moving his family from Haran (12:4–5). But Sarai's faith is not always so clearly stated in the biblical text. It certainly took great faith and courage on Sarai's part to permanently leave her relatives and trek another four or five hundred miles from Haran across desert sands to a far and unknown country. Some may remark that as an Eastern woman of that time period she had no choice in the matter. However, we should note that Sarai often managed matters in her own way, had considerable influence over Abram, and was consulted by him when important decisions were to be made (see 12:11–13). Throughout her life, she appears as a loyal helper to her husband, and her conduct toward him seems always to have been above reproach.

On his journeys, Abram erected an altar to God and called upon the name of the Lord (Genesis 12:7–8; 13:4, 18). This altar may have served primarily to gather his family and servants together for family worship. Here, we discover an important factor in the lives of Abraham and Sarah: they practiced and lived their faith. For her part, Sarah adorned herself with the beauty of contentment and peace due to her faith (1 Peter 3:1–6; see also Hebrews 11:1–2). Lead participants in discussing the importance of home devotions and worship.

21. Because of the famine (v. 10) and the fact that the Canaanites controlled all the good pasture lands (see v. 6), Abram and Sarai were forced to travel into Egypt in order to get grain for their livestock. Even at sixty-five years of age, Sarai was an exceptionally beautiful woman (v. 11). Abram had good reason to fear that an Egyptian might kill him in order to have Sarai. Sarai proved her love for Abram by consenting to his plan. However, both failed to put the matter before the Lord and trust in Him; they would have to learn that God will not forsake His own. God's intervention by sending plagues to Egypt averted a tragedy for Abram and Sarai.

However, because they had given offense by attempting to deceive their hosts, they had to leave the country speedily. Lead participants in discussing the danger of hiding one's religion and playing loosely with moral principles.

22. Sarai and Abram were wealthy. Sarai must have played an important part in helping Abram to manage a large establishment. We learn that there were at least 318 male servants (Genesis 14:14)—and probably also many female slaves—in their home. Sarai must have been a good manager to keep such an enterprise in order. The fact that Abram was honored and respected by the Canaanite chieftains shows that there was something about him and Sarai that made a deep impression upon their unbelieving neighbors. It seems that their longest stay was at Hebron and that here they were held in highest esteem until their death.

Sarai was included in the special promise God gave to Abraham. Abram's offspring would come through her (Genesis 13:15). Through Sarai, her servant Hagar (see 16:10), and Keturah (Genesis 25:1–4; see also 1 Chronicles 1:28–34), God would provide Abram with many physical descendants. All who trust in Christ as the promised Messiah and the world's Savior are the spiritual children of Abraham (Romans 4).

Sarai's Desire for a Child

23. Some participants may be able to identify with Sarai's unfulfilled longing for a child, so approach this discussion with sensitivity and tact. In ancient times, women regarded childlessness as a disgrace. The general custom in those days was for the male head of the household to take additional wives in order to obtain children, so it is curious that Abram had not done this earlier. Sarai and Abram must often have wondered how God's promise of children would ever be fulfilled.

What shall we say about Sarai's suggestion to Abram to marry her Egyptian maid? This incident shows Sarai's impatience at the breaking point. If God would not act, she had to. Providence moved too slowly for her, as it sometimes does for us also. She failed to consider the moral issues at stake and took a step that she was to regret later. Sarai and Abram resorted to measures that were directly contrary to the will of God and evidence of their weak faith (v. 3). As a result, their peaceful and lovely home became disrupted for thirteen years with strife and trouble (v. 5). Before casting stones at Sarai, let us ask ourselves whether we are not often like her. How often are we also impatient with the Lord's work in our lives?

24. Sarai and Abram's rash act eventually caused heartache in their home, resulting in Hagar and Ishmael's expulsion (Genesis 16:4–6; 21:8–13). In order to strengthen their faith and to signify a rise in their status, God changed Sarai and Abram's names. Sarai (probably meaning "contentious") became Sarah (meaning "princess"). This latter name signified that Sarah would be the mother of mighty rulers. Abram (meaning "exalted father") became Abraham ("father of many"). Their son's name would be Isaac.

25. While being very hospitable, Sarah and Abraham were unaware that they were entertaining the preincarnate Son of God (Genesis 18:1, 10, 13, 22) and two of His angels (Genesis 19:1). Christians are enabled to extend hospitality as a sign of God's grace extended to us, and we may even be extending that hospitality (1 Peter 4:9) to strangers, as has happened before. In the past such strangers have sometimes included angels (Hebrews 13:2). Sarah laughed at the Lord's promise, because she thought it ridiculous not only for a woman of her age to conceive and give birth to a child but also for Abraham to be a father (vv. 10–12). The Lord, however, had great patience with Sarah. His gentle rebuke (vv. 13–15) humbled her and restored her through repentance to faith. Hebrews 11:11 assures us of this. Allow participants to discuss those times when we are most likely to doubt God's Word.

Sarah as a Happy Mother

26. Sarah became a mother at the age of ninety. Her laughter of doubt (Genesis 18:12) became a laughter of joy (21:6–7). The birth of Isaac reminds us of the birth of John the Baptist, whose parents Zechariah and Elizabeth (see Luke 1:57) were also older and beyond childbearing years. Children are God's gift (Psalm 113:9), a "heritage" and a "reward" (Psalm 127:3). Allow participants to discuss when they have been overjoyed, to the point of joyful tears or laughter, by God's amazing work in their lives.

27. After sharing marital rights with Hagar for thirteen years, Sarah felt forced to take action to improve her family situation. We cannot say that she dealt fairly and justly with Hagar, but she was justified in considering first the welfare of her young child, Isaac.

Due to the increasing immorality of our contemporary culture, parents often face challenging situations in which they must make difficult choices in the best interests of their children. These could include rigorous monitoring of Internet activity, prohibiting school sports activities that compete with weekend Christian worship times, and so on. Allow participants to discuss other difficult decisions parents must make today on behalf of the children's welfare.

28. We can only imagine that Sarah was obviously concerned about the well-being of her son, Isaac, and overjoyed when both he and Abraham returned safely from worshiping the Lord. Abraham believed in the resurrection of the dead (v. 5) and was confident that, should God go through with His demand that Abraham's son be sacrificed, He could also raise Isaac from the dead. Sarah must have joined Abraham in this belief. Here, we have a beautiful picture of what our heavenly Father would do in the sending of His only-begotten Son to the altar of sacrifice with the wood of the cross on His back. There, Jesus, the Lamb of God provided by God, would suffer and die for the sins of the world. In three days, however, He would rise again.

Sarah's Death and Burial

29. The Bible gives more attention and detail to Sarah's death at 127 years of age and her burial than to that of any other woman. Abraham made elaborate preparations for her burial, placing her as the first one in that famous burial plot. Obviously he grieved for his wife (v. 2), but we must think also that he took comfort in the resurrection in which Abraham and Sarah and all believers will participate on the Last Day. Abraham's purchase of the property for the family burial tombs indicates Abraham's reliance on God's promise that this was to be their ancestral land. In addition to visiting the funeral home or sending a condolence card, allow participants to discuss what they or their congregation can do to help those grieving over a loss.

30. Not Sarah alone, but also Abraham, Isaac, Jacob, Rebekah, and Leah lie at rest in Abraham's tomb until the day of the resurrection. Of course, Isaac was saddened by his mother's death, but his marriage to Rebekah was a source of comfort during this time (Genesis 24:67). Allow participants to read and discuss God's

promise of our bodily resurrection in Job 19:25–27 and Romans 6:3-5.

Other Biblical References to Sarah

31. Isaiah points to Sarah and Abraham as proof of God's faithfulness in keeping His promises to His people. Because they were people of faith in the coming Christ, Sarah and Abraham truly are our spiritual mother and father. Allow participants to discuss other women in their lives who have played a role in their faith development by bringing them to Baptism, reading or teaching them the Scriptures, serving as a spiritual friend or advisor, or so on.

32. According to Paul, Sarah's true children are those who trust in her descendant, our Savior, Jesus Christ. Knowing that we have spiritual mothers and fathers, some of whom have gone before us and some who continue their influence in our lives today, can be a source of encouragement as we see God's mercy and grace operating in their lives. All believers can look forward with great joy to meeting Sarah, Abraham, and all those who have died trusting in Christ on the Last Day.

33. In Paul's allegory in Galatians 4:22–31, Sarah is the "free woman." Her children are not children of the Law, but children of the promise, which is received through faith. Dependence upon the Law for our salvation leads either to self-justification (for presumably fulfilling God's Law, which is impossible for us sinners) or to despair (in recognition that such an effort by us cannot be made). The Gospel, however, the Good News of Christ's perfect obedience, His substitutionary death upon the cross, and His glorious resurrection for us is the fulfillment of the promise. This Gospel, which reveals God's deep love, is what unites us with Sarah and all believers of all times and places. Thanks be to God that we have been set free from the demands of the Law through faith in God's one and only Son!

34. Although both laughed at the thought of conceiving and giving birth to a son, Sarah and Abraham nevertheless had faith and exercised that faith in their lives. Allow participants to discuss those promises in God's Word that are particularly comforting to them and why.

35. Peter extols Sarah as an example of a virtuous wife (1 Peter 3:1–6). Read Galatians 5:22–23, and allow participants to dis-

cuss the fruit of the Spirit that they witness in each other and in other believers in their lives.

Other Women of That Period

36. In spite of the disagreements between her and Sarah, God was nevertheless gracious to Hagar. God promised her a son, although he would have a troubled life. Hagar gave evidence of her faith in God, who undoubtedly appeared to her (v. 13). Ishmael grew up, became an archer, fathered twelve sons, and had a contentious relationship with the family of his half brother, Isaac. Modern Arabs are Ishmael's descendants.

37. Participants may be familiar with the sad story of Lot's wife, who, longing to return to Sodom, turned back after leaving the city and was turned into a pillar of salt (Genesis 19:26). Jesus affirms the historicity of this event (Luke 17:32). Lead participants in a discussion of contemporary temptations for women in particular, but also for Christians in general, and conclude by discussing the strength we have over our temptations through Christ in His Word and Sacraments.

38. The descendants of Lot's daughters included the Moabites and Ammonites, enemies of Israel. Ruth was a Moabite and a legal ancestor of our Savior, Jesus Christ (Ruth 4:21–22; Matthew 1:1, 5–6, 16).

39. According to Paul, a Christian who loses his or her spouse to death is free to remarry (1 Corinthians 7:8–9, 39).

Rebekah

Participants will be blessed studying the life of Rebekah, even though the details of her life may be familiar to them. The story of Rebekah and Isaac provides important lessons regarding the relationships between husbands and wives and between parents and children. Rebekah and Isaac show us why we should believe and trust in God, submit humbly and patiently to His wise providence, and demonstrate a sincere Christian attitude toward all the members of our families.

With the exception of the story of Ruth, the biblical account of Rebekah and Isaac is the most charming story of romance and courtship in the Bible. It presents principles that can guide those who are married or those who are about to be married.

Rebekah's Courtship and Marriage

40. Abraham desired that his and Sarah's son, Isaac, marry. This concern was more than the simple desire for grandchildren; he and Sarah trusted in the Lord's promise that their descendant would be the promised Seed, the Messiah. Abraham and Sarah hoped that Isaac's wife would be a believer. Later, Rebekah and Isaac experienced hardship when their son Esau married unbelieving women (Genesis 26:34–35). Allow participants to discuss the benefits of a common faith between husband and wife.

41. Abraham was worried about two things that he did not want Isaac to do: (1) to marry an unbelieving Canaanite woman and (2) to abandon God's command and promise by leaving Canaan and living in another country only for the sake of a wife. Therefore, he held his faithful servant Eliezer to an oath. Since Abraham had learned about the state of affairs in his brother's family at Haran (Genesis 22:20–24), he was confident that a godly woman could be found there. Eliezer appears to have been well qualified for carrying out his master's wishes; he was a man of strong character, and he was a good judge of people. Moreover, he was a man of strong faith and piety, like Abraham, and relied on God to give success to his mission in answer to fervent prayer

(24:12–14). Ultimately, Eliezer's success lay in God's will and promise to provide a wife and heir who would lead finally to the birth of His Son, Jesus Christ.

42. Eliezer's amazing success points to God's interest in this marriage and how graciously and miraculously He works on behalf of His people. Rebekah was the granddaughter of Abraham's brother, Nahor, and was very beautiful (v. 16). Rebekah's name, which means "rope with a noose," has been interpreted to mean that that her beauty captured men. She was still unmarried, probably because there were no godly men in Haran outside her family. Eliezer quickly learned about Rebekah's family background and her fine character. From this passage of Scripture, we learn that Rebekah was friendly, courteous, humble, kindhearted (even to animals), industrious, and eager to serve. By being both generous and sincere, Eliezer won her confidence and through her gained immediate access to her family.

43. As the messenger of Abraham, Eliezer was a welcome guest in Rebekah's home. Rebekah's parents recognized God's hand in this unusual visit (vv. 50–51). They consented to the marriage. However, they properly left the final decision to Rebekah (vv. 57–58). Rebekah promptly and voluntarily pronounced her "I will."

We can appreciate how hard it was for Rebekah to leave her loved ones. Eliezer realized that this would become harder the longer they delayed. Who can imagine what kind of feelings she had as she traveled those five hundred miles to Beersheba? But Rebekah could be assured of these important facts: she had the prayers and blessings of her parents, she would receive the love and loyalty of a godly husband, and she would enjoy God's blessing upon her married life.

44. In just five verses, the Bible describes the meeting of Rebekah and Isaac and their marriage (vv. 62–67). Isaac seems to have sought the privacy of the desert to pray for the success of the mission and to meet his bride unseen by inquisitive eyes. Rebekah showed a modesty and respect by following the customs of her day, dismounting the camel and covering her face with a veil. The marriage seems to have been a quiet affair, probably performed by Abraham. Moses, the sacred writer, particularly emphasizes Isaac's love for his new bride.

Rebekah as a Wife and Mother

45. For many years, Rebekah and Isaac seem to have lived very happily together. Yet they shared a sorrow that they had to bear for twenty years, that of childlessness. We know how the patriarchs felt about having children. However, Rebekah and Isaac did not lose hope or faith in God, but persistently prayed for the gift of children. Finally God heard their prayer, and Rebekah became the mother of twins. Before their birth, God somehow revealed to Rebekah (Martin Luther suggested that this occurred through Abraham) that He had chosen the younger son to become the bearer of the messianic promise. This did not mean that Esau was to have no share in that promise, but only that God had His own reasons for bestowing greater honor upon the younger son.

46. The fact that Esau and Jacob had different interests does not in itself indicate that the one was good and the other bad. However, they showed differences in temperament and character. Esau seems to have been wild, boisterous, and reckless and to have loved exciting adventure. Jacob was peaceful, retiring, and contemplative, yet secretly he seems to have nurtured the dangerous traits of pride, ambition, and crafty scheming.

It may have been natural, but it was unfortunate, that Isaac and Rebekah showed their partiality openly. Thus both sons were deprived of the affection and influence of one parent. The reason for this favoritism seems to have been that Isaac liked worldly things, such as good, tasty food, whereas Rebekah kept in mind what a great destiny God had decreed for Jacob. In seeking to push Jacob ahead of Esau, she probably encouraged him to take advantage of his flighty brother at every opportunity. Thus he managed to induce Esau to renounce his birthright, which in those days entitled the bearer to become his father's heir and successor. Esau's momentary indifference toward this ancient rule deprived him of rights and privileges that later he was not willing to forfeit (see Hebrews 12:14–17). Allow participants to discuss how contemporary Christian parents can ensure that their time and devotion are spent fairly on their children, particularly in view of special spiritual, emotional, or physical needs of one or more children.

47. Both couples resorted to deception in the fear that a powerful ruler would take the wife. Just as Abraham told Abimelech, king of Gerar, that Sarah was his sister because she was very beautiful,

so, too, did Isaac deceive Abimelech, king of the Philistines, because of his beautiful "sister," Rebekah. Sarah was, of course, Abraham's half sister and Rebekah was Isaac's cousin (first cousin once removed; Rebekah's father, Bethuel, was Isaac's first cousin; Genesis 24:15), a "sister" in Middle Eastern terms. In both cases, the deception was slight. As Abimelech indicated (this may have been a son of the one in chapter 20, both father and son having the same name or the name being a title), Isaac had no reason for playing such a game of deception, because the people of Gerar respected him and his God. Allow participants to discuss how we can and should learn both from our parents' good example as well as their mistakes.

48. Here we have the case of mixed marriages in Rebekah's home, to which we have already referred. The Hittites, of whom very little is known, were a powerful nation of antiquity. For a time they ruled over Egypt and Canaan, but later were driven northward into Asia Minor. Of course, difficulty in tribal customs comes into play, but what is most revealing is that Esau chose women who were from the unbelieving Hittites. When Christians marry outside of the Christian faith, Christian family members are put in a difficult position of sharing family love and acceptance with someone with whom they have no deeper spiritual fellowship. We can only imagine Rebekah and Isaac's predicament. Allow participants to discuss their own experiences in this regard, as well as helpful suggestions they might have for others in a similar predicament.

49. Some devout commentators, including Luther, defend Rebekah and claim that she performed a heroic act of faith in securing for Jacob what rightfully belonged to him. But many scholars today think that she deceived her husband and encouraged Jacob to become a liar and deceiver. As far as we can judge from the story and on moral grounds, Rebekah's conduct was sinful. She may have had mere worldly motives in securing the blessing for Jacob. Rebekah's lack of trust in God led her to try to take matters into her own hands. Instead of waiting for God to provide a way for Jacob to legitimately obtain the coveted blessing, she relied on her own cunning and trickery. Often we are tempted to do the same. Allow participants to discuss what practical, faith-filled steps Rebekah could have taken to resolve this matter in a God-pleasing way.

50. Undoubtedly, all four persons involved were to blame for the tragedy that drove peace and happiness permanently from their

home. Isaac should have remembered what God had said (Genesis 25:23) and should not have been partial to Esau. Esau had proved himself unworthy of the blessing and should have laid no claim to it. Rebekah should have reminded Isaac of God's will and have had the whole affair settled openly. Jacob, of course, should not have obeyed his mother. Whenever we are given orders that conflict with God's Word, we are to obey God rather than people, even if they are in positions of authority over us (Acts 5:29). Allow participants to list other occasions when we must "obey God rather than men."

51. The Bible records the results of their deception (Genesis 27:42–28:5). Jacob had to flee and live in exile for twenty years. Meanwhile, Rebekah died without getting to see her favorite son again. Isaac's remaining years were spent in loneliness. Esau migrated to the country of Edom, south and east of the Dead Sea, but he seems to have remained in touch with his father to his end. While God richly forgives our sins through Christ, He does not always allow us to go without suffering the temporal consequences of them. Nevertheless, our assurance of salvation and forgiveness for all sins lies in our Savior, Jesus Christ. Ask participants to look up Psalm 103:10–12; Ephesians 1:7; and 1 John 4:9–10 and then discuss how our surety of God's forgiveness is based not on our feelings but on His gracious Word of promise in Christ.

52. We hear nothing more of Rebekah except that she lies buried in the cave of Machpelah at the side of Isaac (see Genesis 49:31). Paul mentions her in Romans 9:10. From Rebekah, participants can learn the importance of showing affection fairly to their children (and perhaps grandchildren and other younger relatives) and of relying on God's Word and remaining faithful to it even when it appears things are going against His will. We also learn from her the benefit of being determined, energetic, and quick-acting, as well as that of being kind and sensitive to relatives and strangers. Allow participants to discuss other admirable qualities demonstrated by this foremother in faith.

Other Women of That Period

53. In Genesis 35:8, we learn that Rebekah's nurse was Deborah. Possibly Deborah was Rebekah's nursemaid, assisting her with feeding and nurturing Jacob and Esau. She was an important part of the family, since Jacob named the oak that grew above Deb-

orah's grave *Allon-bacuth*, which means "weeping oak." This is not the Deborah of Judges.

54. Genesis 26:34 tells us about Esau's marriage to two Hittite women and the trouble these women caused. When Esau saw that his parents had turned against him because of his wives, he married a daughter of Ishmael, the half brother of Isaac, believing that his staying within the family might heal the breach. Through this marriage, both Ishmael and Esau became the forefathers of the Arabs. A list of Esau's wives, children, and descendants is given in Genesis 36.

Leah and Rachel

The stories of Leah and her sister Rachel may be familiar to most participants. Some parts of their story need to be handled with wisdom and tact. The purpose of this session is not so much to learn more about Jacob, but to direct participants into study about the two sisters who became his wives. We can assume that Leah and Rachel shared Jacob's faith. It is, of course, difficult to make comparisons between the two sisters and to find notable differences in their characters. Nevertheless, we can learn a lot about ourselves and our families by studying Leah and Rachel.

Leah: Unloved but Full of Praise

55. *Leah* means "cow," while *Rachel* means "ewe." The text makes clear that Leah was less attractive than her younger sister. She had "weak" eyes (v. 17), which probably means that she suffered some sort of eye ailment. Laban probably forced Leah upon Jacob because he feared that no man would want her (greed may have also motivated him). Custom at that time demanded that the bride keep her face veiled on her wedding day, which is why Jacob did not discover Laban's deception until the next day.

The real reason why Jacob did not want Leah was that he was deeply in love with her sister. Jacob resented Laban's trick, but he did not force Laban to abide by the original contract. Perhaps Jacob did not exercise his rights because he remembered how he had treated his father and brother or because he feared that he might lose Rachel in the end. By staying with Leah while continuing to center all his affections on Rachel, he did not treat Leah fairly (vv. 30–31). Allow participants to discuss the many factors today that contribute to unhappiness in the home.

56. God comforted Leah for the wrong she had suffered from her husband by granting her many children. The gift of children brought cheer into her life. Note the names she gave to her sons. When she gave birth to Levi, she hoped that Jacob would become more attached to her. Unfortunately, this was not to be the case.

Ultimately, Leah sought truer companionship and favor from God, her divine Savior, whom she praised.

57. Here again, we witness believers taking unfortunate situations into their own hands, as we saw in Genesis 16. Jacob now had four wives and eventually four sets of children. The incident related in Genesis 30:14–16 illustrates what petty wrangling and scheming the wives indulged in. What kind of fruit the mandrakes were is not definitely known; they were probably regarded superstitiously and believed to stimulate sexual desire and fertility. However, Leah became the mother of three more children not due to the mandrakes, but to the fact that God heard and answered her prayer.

Allow participants to discuss the temptations the devil presents us when we experience strong emotions such as love or anger. What can we do to guard against sinning in those situations?

58. Leah had six sons and one daughter. God later set the children of Levi apart to serve as His priests and have sole charge of public worship. Judah became the ancestor of the leading tribe of Israel, the forefather of David and his royal house, and the bearer of the messianic promise (Genesis 49:10). Levi and his brother Simeon took bloody vengeance and became murderers (Genesis 34). From Genesis 49:31, it is evident that Leah had died before Jacob migrated to Egypt. She was buried by him in Machpelah.

Rachel: Beloved but Unhappy

59. Evidently, Jacob fell in love with Rachel at first sight and continued to love her fervently all his life. Her physical beauty is noted in the Bible (Genesis 29:17). In the Middle East, it was customary for the bridegroom to pay a dowry to the bride's parents, the amount fixed according to the family's station and wealth. Since Jacob, as an exile, had no property, he was obliged to give his bride's parents in labor the equivalent to the sum required. In Jacob's case, this meant seven years of service. From Genesis 29:27–30, it appears that he was permitted to marry Rachel one week after his marriage to Leah, but then he had to work another seven years without wages. Allow participants to discuss whether Jacob is to be blamed for preferring Rachel over Leah or in his actions toward each of them based on that preference.

60. In ancient times, children, and many children at that, were greatly prized. Rachel grieved because her sister had one child after

another. In her disappointment, Rachel finally revealed that she was angry with the Lord for denying her children. She resorted to the common Ancient Near East practice of offering her maid to Jacob. In that day, the maid's offspring would have been considered the offspring of the wife. While not an acceptable moral practice in our day, it was common practice in that culture. In the course of time, Rachel evidently repented of her sinful conduct. Ultimately, God heard her prayer and blessed her with the gift of Joseph (30:22). Allow participants to read and discuss 1 Thessalonians 5:17; John 14:13; and 15:16, which focus on a Christian's devotion to prayer.

61. Laban's "images" were household gods or idols (Genesis 31:19, 30). Although Laban had a certain fear of the Lord (31:29, 53), he also venerated heathen idols and nurtured superstitious beliefs. Rachel apparently was not as yet freed from these vestiges of idolatry. Jacob probably did not learn about this secret idolatry until they had reached Bethel. When he did, he ordered a thorough housecleaning (35:2). Allow participants to discuss how familiar temptations lead so easily into sinful behavior.

62. Sadly, Rachel died giving birth to Benjamin, but not without seeing her newborn son (Genesis 35:16–20). She was buried a little north of Bethlehem. Rachel's sons were always Jacob's favorites; he loved these more than all his other children (Genesis 37:3; 42:4). As the Bridegroom of His bride, the Church, Jesus showed His devotion and love by offering Himself up fully as a sacrifice for her sins and the sins of the whole world (Ephesians 5:24–27).

Other Women of That Period

63. Little is known about these two women. Genesis 37:2 refers to both women as Jacob's "wives," although they were servants to their mistresses, Leah and Rachel. Allow participants to discuss the particular struggles encountered by blended families and the importance of respect and love in them.

64. Shechem, the son of Hamor, a Hivite prince, raped Dinah. The Canaanites were so deplorable that they would even undergo the rite of adult circumcision—thus making a sham of it—in order to intermarry with Israelite women. For the Israelites' part, they too sinned in this by making a sham of covenant circumcision, having "the appearance of godliness" (2 Timothy 3:5). Levi and Simeon,

along with others, killed Shechem, Hamor, and all the men for this grave injustice against their sister, and took all of their possessions. After her brothers committed this act, they took Dinah (Genesis 34:26). We hear no more of her other than a brief mention in Genesis 46:15. Like love, anger is a strong emotion. Neither are sinful in of themselves, but Christians should be wary of allowing emotion to take control of them and of sinning in the process. Ephesians 4:26 makes it clear that we should strive not to sin when we are angry, not that we sin when we experience anger.

65. When Judah says in Genesis 38:26 that Tamar is "more righteous than I," he is stating that Tamar is following the Old Testament principle of levirate marriage. Tamar trusted in the Law of God to provide a means for her to have a child; Judah was trying to circumvent that Law, and Tamar's actions forced him to recognize that. Like Rahab (Matthew 1:5), Tamar was a Gentile included in the household of faith—faith that trusted in the coming Messiah.

66. Potiphar's wife was an example of the low moral standards in Egypt among the rich and mighty. Through faith in Christ, God promises to give us the strength we need when we are faced with even strong temptation (1 Corinthians 10:13). He will provide us a "way of escape."

67. The priest of On was evidently an Egyptian official of high prominence. Owing to Joseph's great influence, some Egyptians probably became believers in the one true God, the God of Abraham, Isaac, and Jacob. It is likely that Asenath became a believer through Joseph's witness and lifestyle. In 1 Corinthians 7:13–15, Paul encourages believing husbands and wives to remain married to their unbelieving spouses, with the prayer, hope, and possibility that they might come to faith ("made holy;" v. 14).